IMAGES OF NORWAY

MEREHURST PRESS
LONDON

IMAGES OF
NORWAY
PHOTOGRAPHY BY
MICK BARNARD
FOREWORD BY
DAVID BELLAMY

PUBLISHED 1988 BY MEREHURST PRESS
5 GREAT JAMES STREET
LONDON WC1N 3DA

© COPYRIGHT 1988 BY MEREHURST LIMITED

ISBN 1 85391 009 0

DESIGN BY SUNSET DESIGN LIMITED

TYPESETTING BY ROWLAND PHOTOTYPESETTING (LONDON) LTD

PRINTED BY NEW INTERLITHO S.P.A. ITALY

THE AUTHOR WOULD LIKE TO THANK THE FOLLOWING
FOR THEIR HELP:

IAN BAIRD OF FRED OLSEN LINES

MAURICE MICHAEL OF LOSTWITHIEL, CORNWALL

JOHAN BERGE, OF THE NORWEGIAN TOURIST BOARD, OSLO

SNORRE EVENSBERGET, OSLO

FINN NYQUIST, OSLO

TORGEIR GARMO, LOM

DR. DAVID BELLAMY

F O R E W O R D   B Y

D A V I D   B E L L A M Y

"THE NORTHERN WAY" is there waiting to be explored by anyone with a sense of real adventure well laced with the purpose of civilization.

Norway is a long thin country spanning the Arctic Circle, a land of 160,000+ lakes and as many islands which make up the western half of the peninsula that is Scandinavia. In shape it resembles a fish whose fjorded tail wafts the warmth of the North Atlantic Drift up into the Arctic Ocean and whose swollen head provides a productive home for more than half of all Norwegians.

For all natural historians it is a place of rugged wonder – an ancient landscape revitalised and prepared by the Ice Age as a fitting home for some 2,000 species of vascular plant. Arctic alpine meadows abloom and abuzz with flowers and insects are circled by birch, willow, pine, aspen, mountain ash and spruce which cloth both mountain slopes and valley sides. Forests which overflow with the succulence of autumn fruits: cran-, blue-, bill-, crow-, cow-, bear- and cloud-, a berry crop which feeds both birds and humans alike. Even the dark depths of the sprucewoods are alive with deep carpets of moss, liverwort and lichen – a fitting home for Moneses uniflora, King Olaf's candlestick and Linnea borealis, the shy twin flower of Linneas himself.

Birds and animals are there too in abundance which are all rejoicing in the wildness of the place – reindeer, elk, wolverine, bear, wolf, lynx, beaver, otter, marten, grouse, partridge and myriad seabirds to name but a few. Perhaps most infamous of all, the Lemming. Lemming's don't commit suicide – there is only one animal stupid enough to do that. The lemmings, like the Vikings of the sagas overcrowded within their homeland, migrate in explosive search for resources new, some die in the attempt, others found new colonies.

Modern Vikings still enjoy their land – fishing, hunting and farming. Some still sail the seas, masters of navigation, while others show the world the way in good labour relations and small business practice in the commercial and service fields.

These fine pictures capture the essence of it all, challenging you to launch out and let the ice-free warmth of fjordland welcome you into the wonder of "The Northern Way".

DAVID BELLAMY
The Conservation Foundation

TO MY PARENTS

I N T R O D U C T I O N   T O

IMAGES OF NORWAY

THE ANCIENT NORSEMEN believed that the world they inhabited was created from the body of a primaeval giant, conceived in chaos and slain by the gods. His blood formed the seas, his flesh became the earth and the mountains and rocks were made from his bones and teeth.

It is easy to understand the appeal of this imagery when looking at the Norway of today. This is a land where nature still dominates man like the giant of legend. Rugged mountains rear up to overawe the eye. Trackless moorlands stretch endlessly to the horizon, broken by countless lakes and streams. Deep pine forests cover a fifth of the land. Everywhere the bony structure of the giant shows clearly through a tattered cloak of soil.

If the landscape with its impressive glaciers providing mute witness is insufficient to convince the visitor of nature's hold over the Norwegians then a northern climate of extreme temperatures should provide the final evidence of man's need to battle annually against the elements.

Although the population of Norway has more than doubled this century it still totals only a little more than four million people. If the land were to be evenly spread between the population each Norwegian would own 100,000 square metres.

The land has never given much to its people with less than three per cent of Norway being suitable for cultivation. Mining of iron, silver, copper and other ores is important in certain areas of the country but the vast forests still represent an important source of income to the many farmers as a supplement to their animal husbandry. In recent times the very nature of Norway has been harnessed to provide the hydro-power which is such a crucial factor in today's Norwegian prosperity.

The country, however, is only habitable throughout its length because of the warming Gulf Stream that flows all along its western shores, moderating the temperature and keeping ports ice-free throughout the year.

Most Norwegians live on or near the coast, along that sea-borne "Way to the North" – *Nordvegr* – which gave the country its name. Numerous bays and deeply-indented fjords give Norway a shoreline roughly 21,000 km long, not counting the 50,000 islands large and small that fringe the mainland.

Fishing has always been a richer and more reliable source of food than the scarce fields, and becomes increasingly important in the local economy the further north one goes. Shipping remains a major source of jobs and exports, and the oil and gas of the North

Sea have recently fuelled a further improvement in living standards.

Norway's very existence as a nation depends on the watery highway that allowed a series of communities divided by high mountains and glaciers to be welded into a whole during the Viking era more than a millenium ago. Occupying the western side of the great Scandinavian peninsula, the country looks firmly outward to the wide windy wastes of the North Atlantic. In former times, hard bitten Norwegian seamen colonised the remote islands of this ocean – the Faeroes, Iceland, Greenland, reaching as far as North America – and ruled a mediaeval maritime empire that spanned the full breadth of these northern waters.

The high ridge of mountains that marks the boundary with Sweden to the east is known as the Keel – a highly appropriate image for this seagoing nation.

And the country does look in some respects like a longship turned upside down. Also resembling a teaspoon, it stretches over 1752 km from south to north as the crow flies, but measures less than seven km across at its narrowest. Long land distances have always been a fact of Norwegian life. Europe's E6 highway, which runs from Rome to the far north of Norway, has Oslo at its approximate mid-point and runs for more than half its 5,100 km length on Norwegian soil.

If the 13 degrees of latitude covered by Norway north to south equals the distance from the southern tip of the country to central Italy, the span from east to west is equally impressive. The easternmost point is on the same meridian as Leningrad and Istanbul, while its western extremity lies in line with Rotterdam – a time spread of 105 minutes.

At the same time, Norway's inverted hull straddles the Arctic Circle and extends far into the region of the Midnight Sun in summer – and perpetual night during the long winters. And far to the north lie the remote and savage Svalbard islands – the "cold coast" on the edge of the Arctic Ocean that was named Spitzbergen by the Dutch for its many sharp-pointed peaks.

Strong natural forces have shaped the Norwegian landscape. The bedrock consists largely of ancient mountains and volcanoes ground down almost to their roots. These tough rocks were later tilted along the western edge of the country when America tore off from Europe to create the North Atlantic. Rivers cut down through the uplifted massifs to create deep dales flowing to the chilly northern sea.

Then came the ice, covering Norway in a vast sheet that carved existing valleys into deep, U-shaped troughs, scoured the rocks and deposited heaps of debris across the country as boulder-filled moraines. The ice cap only retreated fully some 10,000 years ago, leaving a raw, scraped land that still bears an unfinished look.

This history underlies the contrast between drama and quiet in Norway's scenery. A long chain of ice-worn islands and rocks fringe its shores, battered by wind and waves but also protecting the mainland from the worst effects of Atlantic storms. Behind these skerries in the west, cliffs as sheer as battlements rise sharply from narrow coastal flatlands or direct from the sea. Deep, sombre fjords and level-bottomed valleys cut far into the land, hemmed in by steep walls of naked rock. Rivers are short and filled with rapids, cascading over cliffs as mighty waterfalls. This is *Vestlandet*, home of independent-minded small scale farmers and fishermen.

Once the upthrust western barrier has been scaled, Norway's south-central uplands present vast rolling vistas of rock, lake, moor and glacier ice. Few steep peaks rise from this mountain plateau – the tallest, Galdhøppigen, is only 2,469 metres above sea level. Grazing their animals on the fringes of these highlands and hunting game across their empty, treeless spaces, Norwegians of old conceived them as the fortress home of giants – *Jotunheimen*.

Running east to west, the Dovre mountains mark the northern boundary of these wide wastes, while the whole massif slopes eastwards and southwards towards a gentler and more fertile countryside. A series of huge valleys penetrate far into the highlands from the south-east like the fingers in some vast glove, with the wrist opening out in the region around Oslo that formed the home of Norway's first kings and is the most densely-populated part of the country today.

The great eastern valleys of *Østlandet* are one of the heartlands of Norwegian culture and traditions. Although shaped by the glaciers and fringed by steep-sided cliffs, these valleys are broader and shallower than those in the west. Once the waterfalls have emptied from the plateau, rivers here are longer and slower and include the Glomma, Norway's longest waterway. The farms are larger and more prosperous, with extensive forests of pine and spruce that created the basis for long-established industries. Here was the home of a distinctive rural culture celebrated in the folk tales collected by Asbjørnsen and Moe in the 19th century, and preserved in historic wooden buildings and artefacts.

The highlands extend down into the southern bulge of the country, but the fjords along the south-east coast are more open and less haunting than their majestic brethren of the west. Sørlandet – the south country – is a coast of small, white painted towns with strong shipping traditions, backed by forested hills leading into the mountains proper. During the summer, this is Norway's premier vacation-land, a paradise of cabins and boats, swimming and sunbathing. But the lakes and wide open spaces of the highlands also have their holiday partisans, while the mountains reign supreme for leisure activity during the winter.

On the south-west coast, the low, worn hills of Dalane support Norway's greatest sheep populations and give way to the broad Jæren plain that stretches up towards Stavanger and the beginning of the western fjordlands. Fringed with the country's best sandy beaches, this fertile undulating landscape is criss-crossed by low stone walls built from boulders dragged from the clay soil by generations of toiling farmers.

Across the Dovre mountains to the north lie the broad wooded plains and wide fjords of Trøndelag, one of Norway's historic regions and a major centre for farming and forestry today. Beyond these open landscapes, the Keel comes close to the sea and the barren mountains march with the coast for many hundreds of miles. This *Nordland* landscape is wilder and more jagged than the western fjords, but the islands, the narrow strip of coastal plain called the strandflat, and the valleys provide sites for settlement.

Finally, the bulge of the great Finnmark plateau in the far north provides another region of rolling highland – Europe's last great wilderness, sparsely populated by Lapps and their reindeer herds and cut through by mighty rivers and fjords. Fishing and mining provide occupations for the small isolated communities that dot these magnificent but fundamentally inhospitable shores.

The interaction of sea, land and latitude gives each of these landscapes their characteristic climate. Along the western shores, warmed by the Gulf Stream, abrupt cliffs intercept wet winds rolling in from the Atlantic and cause them to release their water in torrents of rain and snow. This leaves less rainfall for the lands further east in the shadow of the mountains, which are drier and colder. Farmers in the eastern valleys often have to irrigate their

lands during the warm summers, while Norway's winter temperatures are at their lowest along the border with Sweden not far north of Oslo. Thanks to the benign influence of the sea, the city of Tromsø astride the 70th parallel has a milder winter than Oslo 10 degrees further south.

In this far northern land, however, the movement of the sun through the seasons is well marked and plays a crucial role. Months of darkness and cold in the winter give way to endless days in the summer, when the shortness of the growing period is compensated by a perpetual or near-perpetual absence of night. Spring comes with a rush and departs as quickly, the land bursting into fruitfulness with lush exuberance. Autumn is also brief and extremely beautiful, a time when the country takes on a mantle of reds and browns and golds before succumbing to the stark grip of winter. Only the western coast stays green – if sodden – all the year round, and even there snow is just a short climb away on the nearby plateau.

These influences are reflected in Norway's vegetation. Naked rock along the weather-beaten coast gives way in the far south to mixed woodland of deciduous and evergreens. The highlands are largely treeless heath and bog, while the sheltered valleys of the west can support blooming apple orchards as well as the birch and pine that grows so densely in the east and Trøndelag. Further north, only dwarf birch copes well with the rigours of a sub-Arctic climate, along with reindeer moss and other tundra plants on the Finnmark plateau.

Animal life is varied – elk and deer in the forests, reindeer both tame and wild on the highlands, birds everywhere. Many cliffs along the western and northern coasts are crammed with feathered life, providing a noisy home for puffins, gulls, gannets, fulmars and other species. The rivers are well stocked with fish making them a paradise for anglers.

Over many generations, Norwegians have developed a close affinity for their beautiful but largely barren land. They are not an urban people, although their cities and towns have expanded greatly over the past four decades of growing prosperity. A deep sense of the elemental strength and intractability of nature is reflected in the folk tales that still exercise a powerful hold over the Norwegian imagination.

These stories people the mountains and forests of Norway with huge trolls and other monsters representing the mindless cruelty of natural forces. But many tales note that the troll is essentially stupid, and can be outwitted my men and women prepared to meet nature on its own terms with courage, wit and generosity – and sometimes a little help from magic.

Norwegians have also learned how to make the best use of the scanty resources at their disposal, taming the landscape and moulding it to their needs. Centuries of close association with the land and the sea have given them a deep love of the land and a sensitive feel for the natural materials it yields.

A cool, wet climate and hilly fields has always encourged livestock farming. Cattle, sheep and goats were the basis of rural prosperity in former times, supplemented all along the coast with the silver harvest of the seas. Butter, cheese, dried meat and salted fish filled the wooden storehouses that stood on carefully erected

pillars of stone to discourage the rats and mice. More recently, potatoes ranked as the most important crop on many holdings.

Norwegian farmers have always needed to keep their animals under cover during the winter. As water has always been in plentiful supply, the prime consideration in locating farm buildings was to shorten the distance that fodder had to be carried to the barn. This produced a characteristic settlement pattern based on dispersed farms dotted around the countryside with their white painted shelters with black roofs, seen all over rural Norway, standing isolated in the fields. The Norwegian language has lacked its own word for "village" in the European sense, referring instead to "rural districts" or "townships" as the Americans understand them. Expressions for such rural centres have been borrowed from Danish or Swedish as they became increasingly common in the wake of sweeping population shifts since the Second World War.

Only along the northern shores were settlements resembling villages to be found, but these were more in the nature of transient camps where fishermen from along the whole length of the coast congregated for the great seasonal fisheries. Their rude cabins have now been converted to romantic holiday homes, forgetting the hard lives of those who once occupied them.

In modern times, agricultural policies aimed at encouraging self-sufficiency mean that many farmers have turned to growing grain or fodder crops, altering the traditional landscape. The old system of moving animals up to mountain pastures during the summer to make maximum use of available resources has also been largely abandoned – along with romantic stories of courting the maids left on these *saeter* to guard the beasts.

Another trend wreaking great changes in the countryside is the flight from the land. This move parallels similar developments

elsewhere, but has been even more significant in a landscape so previously thinly peopled.

Historically, the flat lands in the valley bottoms were occupied first. Settlement then spread progressively higher up the valley slopes or into less favoured sites, creating a patchwork of smallholdings that were barely enough to support a family. Norway is the only country in Europe to measure the size of its farms in decars – a quarter of an acre or one-tenth of a hectare – because many were so tiny. A growing number of these sites have now been abandoned, the land added to other farms and the buildings converted to holiday cabins or allowed to collapse.

Naturally, such depopulation is particularly acute along the margins of the settled areas and the island communities off the coast where people have felt cut off from the benefits of 20th century life. If the earlier image of travel in the Norwegian coastlands was the ferry and the quay, today's symbol is the bridge and the metalled road – often blasted through solid rock to reach isolated townships.

Although the Norwegian mountains yield stone and the raw materials for cement, the greatest resource available to Norwegians historically has been the timber from their forests.

Wooden artifacts are everywhere in Norway – buildings roofed in turf or tiles, boats, furniture, utensils, fences. The Vikings cheerfully challenged the oceans in their sturdy, flexible longships, intricately carved and decorated. The same love of ornamentation can be seen in the unique stave churches which rank as some of the world's oldest timber structures. Their strange, pagoda-like appearance conceals a core constructed like a longship turned upside-down – a method familiar and natural to the builder in mediaeval Norway. Assembled today in folk museums – a form of preserving the past in open-air collections that was invented in Norway – old farm buildings display a continuing skill in working with wood down the generations. Even today, most Norwegians live in timber houses carefully designed and built to combat the rigours of a northern climate.

These are the images of Norway today – a land shaped by man but not under his full control even now. A land of sunshine and storm, fertile summer and harsh winter, sparkling sea and barren upland, comfortable farmlands and silent forest. A land where the giants continue to rule their mountain fastnesses and trolls still walk a pace or two behind your shoulder.

▲▶

Idyllic Brevik on the Telemark coast is one of Norway's best preserved coastal towns. It is a delight to wander along its fascinating narrow streets between charming gabled buildings that date from the eighteenth and nineteenth centuries.

▲

Surrounding hills clothed in wooded slopes make the Flatdal valley near Nutheim one of Telemark's most beautiful farming areas. The district is famous for intricate carved timberwork as well as for the attractive 'rose painting' that ornamented so many 'bygones' during a great flowering of peasant art two to three hundred years ago.

▶

Small farms exist in areas of cleared forest on the hilly slopes near Haukeligrend, and the surrounding woodland supplies all their firewood and timber needs. Those farmers who actually own large areas of the forest often find that timber is more profitable than agriculture.

◀

Many artists are inspired to try to capture on canvas the charm of these colourful fjord villages, each with its own small harbour. This is picturesque Sand on the south-west coast.

▶

The spectacular two-channelled Latefoss waterfall near the town of Odda is a mecca for tourists in the Hardanger area. This picture shows only part of it, but the length of the total falls is an amazing 400 m (1,300 feet). They thunder down over sheer grey rocks in a breathtaking cascade 165 m (542 feet) deep.

▲

Also near Odda is the Buar valley at the head of Sorfjorden, an arm of that most romantic of all fjords, Hardangerfjorden. In springtime the shores of Sorfjorden dance with pink and white orchard blossom. By paying a small toll at Buar farm, walkers can follow a track through the peaceful valley towards the sun-splashed slopes of the Buar glacier.

▲

The Buar glacier, seen here from high up its valley, is truly fantastic, but it is small compared with the mighty Folgefonn glacier of which it is only an arm. The Folgefonn is the third largest icefield in Norway, about 33 km (20 miles) long and 16 km (10 miles) across at its widest point. It dominates the landscape above the Sorfjorden.

▲

Looking towards the Lysefjorden, near Stavanger on the south-west coast. This sound extends some 44 km (26 miles) into the mountains which are home for the southernmost herds of wild reindeer. In places like the famous flat-topped Pulpit Rock, the bare cliffs plunge vertically downwards for nearly 609 m (2,000 feet) into the fjord below.

▶

Ferries play an important part in the transport system of western Norway: they link the roads severed by those magnificent fjords that indent one of the world's most ragged – and rugged – coastlines. This boat is crossing the beautiful blue Veafjorden to reach the village of Stamnes cradled in its exquisite setting of wood and rock and distant mountain.

▲

Near Voss (one of Norway's largest tourist resorts, winter and summer alike) the enchanting Tvinnefoss waterfall cascades in a perfect fan shape over a series of natural steps – all framed by the delicate tracery of birch trees.

▶

Mist and cloud, pierced by occasional shafts of brilliant sunlight, overshadow Gudvangen at the head of Naeroyfjorden. A journey by ferry along this spectacular sound, dominated by towering mountains of 1066 m (3,500 feet) which are ribboned with tumbling waterfalls, is an unforgettable experience.

▲

The Borgund stave church, dating from about 1150 AD, is considered the best preserved and most typical of Norway's 25 extant stave churches. These masterpieces of late Viking carpentry skill were constructed entirely of timber. Probably 750 churches existed at one time, but, not surprisingly, many fell victim to the ever-present fire hazard – as the modern, red "no smoking" notice reminds us!

▲

Hopperstad stave church, built about 1150 AD, at Vik on Sognefjorden is typical with its shingled roof and decorated ridges. The churches are named after the staves (poles) used in their construction, and their gables and spires are ornamented with the same fang-tongued dragons that formed the prows of Viking longships.

This magnificent piece of architecture is the Staveloft at the Hallingdal folk museum in Nesbyen. Experts consider it possibly the purest styled and most monumental structure of its kind in Norway today. These buildings were storehouses, constructed of rough hewn logs so massive that they have withstood the onslaught of time for many centuries. The Staveloft bears unmistakable traces of its great age – it was built before the Black Death ravaged Norway in 1349.

Norwegian fjord horses are not only beautiful but friendly and fond of company. Their stocky build makes them tireless and hardworking, and small farmers still use them for hauling timber or haycarts.

▲

High altitude pasturing of animals is known in Norway as 'seter' farming. It uses grazing areas above the tree line or in remote forest clearings which are only accessible during the summer. Although on the decline, seter farming is still practised in some areas. The 'seter' cabins in the photograph nestle in the lovely summer valley of Kvammadalen above Aurland.

▲

In late autumn the sun's rays are too weak to disperse the cold mists in the valleys, but this summer farm bathed in early morning sunshine enjoys a cold but sunny day.

▲

The broad and picturesque Valdres valley near Leira is typical of Norway's eastern landscape. Thick forests are pierced by winding rivers and countless lakes (an angler's paradise). The wide valleys are separated by mountain plateaux with gently undulating moorland.

▲

Early October at Fagernes in the Valdres valley, and the brilliant sun picks out the autumn colours of the birches, highlighting them against the dark green of the thick pine forests. In wintertime Fagernes becomes a bustling ski resort, the main centre for the region.

▶

It is early summer at Lake Helgeset in the Hallingdal valley. The sun is already breaking through the silvery morning mist – a good omen for a perfect day ahead.

▲

The Flamsdal valley is an area of exceptional natural beauty, even for Norway. A unique way to experience it is by travelling on the famous Flam mountain railway, which winds its way upward from the valley floor, and climbs to an altitude of 721 m (2,367 feet) in just over 12 miles. At one point on its journey up the mountain the train stops to let passengers admire the Kjosfoss waterfall.

▲

Flam at the head of Aurlandsfjorden, an arm of the great Sognefjorden, is set amid stunning mountain and fjord scenery. It is the starting point for the Flam mountain railway, a spectacular journey through steep-sided, lush-green valleys, towering mountains draped in snow, and tumbling waterfalls.

▶

Snow-capped mountains plunging almost sheer into the blue waters of Aurlandsfjorden near Aurlandsvangen – irrefutable proof of the saying that Norway's fjords are 'Nature at her most magnificent', as they cleave their way through a landscape of incredible grandeur created during the Ice Age.

▼

This derelict log cabin, its turf roof starred with flowers and ferns, looks across Aurlands-fjorden to Flam and its waterfalls. Deserted by its former owners, the building has taken on a new role as a nesting site for the birds which visit Norway in summer.

▲

Norway's greatest sound, the Sognefjorden, seen here by Hermansverk, thrusts its way inland for 210 km (127 miles). The sides of its accompanying mountain peaks can drop from a height of 1600 m (5,250 feet) into the fjord below. Even the largest cruise liners can enter these fjords, which attain depths of 1300 m (4,293 feet) deep in places.

▲

Each fjord has its own character and atmosphere, but Innvikfjorden is one of Norway's most beautiful. The ever-changing light on its tranquil waters creates those special scenes that only the moods of nature can provide.

◄

At the head of the Romsdalsfjorden, dwarfed by a backdrop of jagged snow-capped peaks, sits Andalsnes. Nearby, at Horgheim in the Romsdal valley, looms the famous Trollveggen or 'Troll Wall', 1000 m (3,300 feet) of sheer rock, perhaps Europe's most demanding precipice for top climbers.

▲

A magnificent view, equalled by few (if any) others in Europe, is that of Geirangerfjorden from the summit of Mount Dalsnibba. Four of Norway's most important mountain regions can be seen from this pinnacle, 1500 m (4,907 feet) above sea level. From this direction winter snows cut off the farming valleys below with their meandering rivers and patchwork fields, and it is then that the ferries play their vital role in keeping communications open.

▲

Perhaps the most photographed view in all Norway is this of Geirangerfjorden from Flydalsjuvet. Norway's most dramatic fjord is actually only a small arm of the much larger Storfjorden, but its scenic beauty is so unparalleled that for over a century cruise ships from around the world have visited it in practically all seasons.

▲

The mountains surrounding Geirangerfjorden exceed 1600 m (5,250 feet). Most of their steep flanks, hung with fronds of wild flowers and laced with waterfalls, leave little room for roads or villages. But a few intrepid farmsteads do manage to cling to the barely accessible slopes near the head of the fjord, their occupants scraping a living from the few hundred square yards of soil deposited there.

▲

The awesome scale of the mountains around the wild Isterdal valley near Andalsnes makes the buildings and cars below look like toys. The famous Trollstig road (the 'Troll's path') zigzags vehicles down into the canyon in the centre of the picture.

◄

It is early June in Videdalen, but the snow still lies thick. The spectacular mountain scenery was as great a tourist attraction when the Strynfjell mountain road was opened to horse and carriage in 1895. Today the nineteen hairpin bends are the same, only the vehicles have changed.

▲

Late September on a 'seter' below the Trollheimen mountains near Oppdal. This summer farm's attractive turf makes a strong and lasting cover for its log walls. The roof has to slope at just the right angle – too flat, and rainwater will collect and saturate the grass; too steep, and it will drain too quickly for grass to grow, the turf cracking during dry weather.

◄

Eagle's eye view of the Trollstig as its eleven stomach-churning bends loop down step by step through wild scree and lichen-covered rocks to the Isterdal valley far below. Halfway down, the road, looking like a skein of grey wool reeled off by a giant troll, traverses the thundering force of the Stigfoss waterfall.

▶

A watery sun pierces the clouds above Djupvatnet lake lying 1005 m (3,300 feet) above the Geirangerfjorden. Each winter brings heavy falls of snow, so the nearby Djupvass ski lodge is able to hold ski races well into June. Indeed, often the ice on the lake does not melt until August, yet is frozen over again by November!

▲

Birch trees in their glowing autumn colours of orange and gold brighten the shores of Lake Gjevilvatn. The rough road entices walkers onwards to the tourist cabin Gjevilvasshytta, a starting point for exploring the Trollheimen mountains in the distance.

▶

Under the piercing spotlight of the sun, the vivid autumn livery of birch trees stands out sharply against the looming black storm clouds.

▲

Hafslo, with its scattering of white-painted gables, is a picturesque farming region near the shores of Lustrafjorden. The area is the gateway to some of Europe's most rugged mountains and finest glaciers, found within a short distance in any direction from this tranquil scene.

▲

It is late September in Norddal, where rowan and birch trees splash the lush green of its high mountain valley with scarlet and gold. By now most tourists have abandoned this mountain playground, leaving it to the peace and quiet of nature until the following year.

▶

Over a long period of time the snout of an advancing glacier pushes forward an end moraine and also buries itself in the ground. If the climate warms up, the icefield retreats, melt water accumulates in the depression it leaves behind, and a lake is formed – like this one below the Nigardsbreen glacier.

▲

The snout of Nigardsbreen. Care must be taken when exploring the area around the entrance to a glacier cave: without warning large chunks of ice weighing many tons may break off the slowly advancing icefield. This forward movement cannot be detected by eye, but is confirmed by the ice debris below the cave. Best to observe it from a safe distance!

◄

The Nigardsbreen outlet glacier is one of 24 'tongues' extending from the great Jostedals-bre plateau glacier. Two to three hundred years ago the advance of Nigardsbreen and its sister 'tongues' caused damage to the sur-rounding farmland and houses. Since then the ice has retreated and a wealth of brilliant flowers, shrubs and grasses carpets the valley floor.

◀

Ice formations on the Nigardsbreen glacier.

▲
▶
Even though it is late June, ice still lingers on Jotunheimen's lakes, and snow clings to its craggy slopes. The early part of the month is the best time for dramatic, snow sculptured scenery, but August and September are better for mountain walking. Then the area is clear of excess snow, which no longer treacherously conceals the frozen streams and lakes.

Sognefjell is the highest mountain pass in Norway, 1429 m (4,690 feet) above sea level, with some of the wildest scenes in Jotunheimen. Cairned trails will take hikers through this rugged landscape in relative safety, so long as they take the usual precautions with clothing and equipment suitable for mountain terrain. Mount Fannaraken is seen in the distant background.

◄

A distant view of Galdhopiggen, Norway's highest mountain at 2469 m (8,103 feet). By crossing the Styggebreen glacier, it can be reached in about three hours from the mountain chalet Juvasshytta.

►

Superb panoramic views are the reward for scaling the highest peaks of Jotunheimen.

▲

Winter grips these ice-sculptured gorges and boulder-strewn summits for eight months of the year, with frost on an average of 300 days!

▶

Awe-inspiring snow walls are a great tourist attraction when the Sognefjell mountain road is re-opened in early June. But admiring travellers are advised not to linger too long between these breathtaking thirty-foot walls: often the spring thaw collapses whole sections onto the road.

The mountains, sub-alpine birch belt and lower forested valleys of Jotunheimen are home to a rich display of flora and fauna.

▲

The creamy-white Glacier buttercup, with its corona of yellow stamens, grows among other similarly hardy vegetation high up in the mountains near the snow line. It is a delicacy for reindeer.

▶

The Purple saxifrage makes a regal splash of colour among rock and scree. It is among the hardiest of the flowers found above the tree line.

▼

The exquisite white petals, delicately flushed with mauvish-pink, of the Pale pasque flower are found in high alpine meadows.

▶

The Livelong saxifrage prefers any area where the rocky outcrops to which it clings are found.

▶

Looking not unlike an underwater coral reef, the glowing red autumnal leaves of the Black bearberry contrast brilliantly with the abundant yellow Reindeer moss (actually a lichen). Both are found on moors, mountains and open forest areas.

◄

The purple Wood cranesbill flourishes in forests and sheltered pockets on the mountainside.

◄

White bracts surrounding purplish-black flowers crown the vividly mottled, oval green leaves of the Dwarf cornel. It can be found over a wide range of habitats – from birch woods to heaths, moors and mountains.

▲

Ptarmigan are found in mountains, normally above the treeline. They change their plumage to match the seasons – this cock bird is in its mottled coat of early spring.

▶

The beautiful Dotterel nests on tundra and mountains. A very trusting bird, with care it can be approached quite closely. This bird's mate can just be discerned against the snow bank in the background.

▲

Reindeer trek along a snow bank in the Jotunheimen mountains. In summer, these animals move up onto the windy ridges and snow fields to keep cool and to escape the flies that plague them in the lower valleys.

▶

The colourful, hamster-like Lemmings are common all over Norway's mountain region and, in 'lemming years', when numbers increase dramatically, they can be found right down to the fjords. Lemmings are also the key to the breeding success of birds of prey such as owls, buzzards and falcons, whose chick numbers increase or decrease in proportion to the lemming population.

▼

A female European elk feeding on pond vegetation. This impressive animal, largest member of the deer family, can weigh up to 550 kg (1,200 lb) and measure 2.13 m (7 feet) at the shoulder.

◄

Red deer can be seen in many of Jotunheimen's forested valleys. The splendid antlers of the male (stag) are shed and regrown annually.

▲

Both wild and partially controlled herds of Reindeer wander vast distances searching for food. They can be seen in forested areas well away from the mountains, though they are equally heavily dependent there on lichens for food, especially in winter.

▲

Wolverines seldom visit Jotunheimen, but are found in many other locations. They wander into mountain areas that have easy access to nearby forests. Very powerful predators for their size, they can even kill sick or injured Reindeer, as well as eating carrion, small animals and birds.

▲

Unless Brown bears had wandered in from another area, they would be a rare sight in Jotunheimen. A few do still exist in some areas of Norway, though they are scarcely ever seen, being very wary and fleeing at the first scent of humans. They will eat anything – from berries and grass (on which they graze like cows) to carrion and all sorts of small animals and birds, as well as larger creatures like deer.

▲

This view across Volbufjorden in Oystre Slidre, with buildings dotting the landscape, is typical of the farming regions surrounding Jotunheimen. In the distance can be seen the mountains around Bygdin. Jotunheimen's south-east entrance.

◀

Here the rapids of the Sjoa river churn their way through narrow rock-edged channels fringed by the pine forest at Ridderspranget. All Sjoadalen's lakes and rivers offer good fishing for trout and red char. Peace and solitude are a treasured part of Norway's fishing scene.

▲

The toll roads found throughout Norway penetrate mountain and forest areas not normally accessible to motorists. These roads also make excellent routes for walkers (who are not charged any toll). This track through Kakelldalen gives a wonderful view of the distant mountains in the Rondane National Park.

▲

Looking from Faldet farm in the beautiful Grimsdal valley over the north-eastern edge of the Rondane National Park. Wild reindeer, wolverine and red fox live here, otter and mink are found in the meandering waterways, and elk wander majestically through the forested valleys surrounding the park.

▶

A tranquil farming scene, dotted with red and white cabins and delicate birch trees, is reflected in the limpid waters of the River Glomma near Mount Tron in the Osterdal valley.

◄

The gorgeous oranges and yellows of the setting sun are mirrored here in Lake Femund in the district of Engerdal. Almost 560 m (2,000 ft) above sea level, and covering some 21,000 hectares (80 square miles), the lake lies close to the Swedish border. Its north-eastern shore runs alongside the Femund-smarka National Park. This wilderness of pine forest, bare mountains and numerous lakes is home to reindeer and the occasional wolver-ine, lynx, elk, mink and beaver.

▲

The romantic old town of Roros near the Swedish border, at 800 m (2,630 ft) above sea level, shivers between December and February in temperatures below −30°C (−22°F). The octagonal white church, outlined in black, is the only stone building in the old section of the town. It was built as long ago as 1784, and the crossed mining tools above each of the clock faces on its tower remind visitors of the town's former trade.

▲

The ancient streets of Roros are lined with enchanting historic buildings – elegant houses, painted peach, white and grey, with delicately ornamented lintels. Whole streets unchanged by time truly justify the town's place on UNESCO's world heritage list.

▲

Slaggveien, a seventeenth-century street in Roros, boasts charming, timber-built miners' cottages, with small-paned windows and turf roofs. From their old chimneys wood smoke drifts nostalgically into the tranquil air.

▶

Snow can fall in Norway as early as October, and often lingers in lowland areas until April. Many of the high mountains passes may not be clear until July. This is late November, a time when the forest is transformed into picturesque Christmas card scenes.

▲

Snowmobile tracks cut across the crisp cover of pure white snow in this valley near Tyin.

▶

It is late November and this summer farm is deserted for the winter. The low sun may touch the tips of the mountain above its forest cloak, but will have no effect on the sub-zero temperatures.

◄

A cold, still November day in Ottadalen. The wonderful reflection of snow-capped mountains will quickly disappear as ice creeps out from each bank and eventually covers the sluggish waters of the Otta river.

▲

Gressamoen National Park in North Trondelag was designated in 1970 to protect an area of primaeval spruce forest and the mountain and woodland areas of inner Trondelag. However, accessibility is not easy, since the park has no marked trails or tourist huts. Many shy animals take advantage of its solitude – reindeer, lynx, red fox and pine marten. Bird life includes golden eagles and gyrfalcons.

◄

It is early May, and the slow thaw is beginning. It starts first on the road with traffic use, but it is only very gradually that the giant icicles draping the banks succumb to the advancing warmth of the spring.

▼

The small village of Skarstad crouches on the beautiful wild coast of Ofotfjorden at latitude 68°22′ north. Such settlements in the far north can survive only by a combination of fishing and farming.

▶

Some of the finest coastal scenery is found on the Lofoten Islands: this deserted rock-strewn beach surrounded by jagged cliffs is at Utakleiv on Vestvagoy.

◄

The jagged peaks of the Lofoten Islands rise like sentinels from the surrounding waters of Vestfjorden. These dramatic islands extend for more than 215 km (129 miles) from east to west in a line south-west of Narvik. They are a centre for fishing fleets, a haunt of seabirds and a magnet for climbers.

▲

This farm near the fishing village of Eggum is dwarfed by its magnificent surroundings of craggy mountains. On Vestvagoy enough pastureland enriches the mountains for many sheep to be grazed there, along with goats and cows for milk. Indeed, farming is now as important as fishing in terms of employment and turnover.

▲

Austnesfjorden on Austvagoy in the Lofotens,
a typical scene with fishing boats anchored off
the village, and steep mountains plunging
down to the ice-blue fjord.

▶

Looking across Salangen Sound towards the incredibly pointed mountains on the island of Andorja off the rugged north-west coast.

▼

The Vesteralen is a cluster of remarkable islands, 200 km (120 miles) north of the Arctic Circle. They follow on from the Lofoten Islands in a north-easterly direction, separated by a narrow sound and the wide Hadselfjorden (shown here).

◄

It is late May and new leaves on the birch trees hint at the coming of spring. Already in this far northern village of Dalen, latitude 68°52', daylight lasts around the clock.

▲

Conifers grow all the way up to the far north of Norway, but as here at Fisklausvatn, some 300 km (180 miles) north of the Arctic Circle, they are very stunted due to the growth-inhibiting factors of this northerly location.

▶

On this glorious day in early June, near Kviteberg farm on the bleak and barren sub-Arctic coast of Kvaenangen, the snow-covered peaks of Kvaenangtindene beckon enticingly across the fjord.

▶

Langfjorden lies just north of the 70th parallel. On cold windless days in early June, the snow-covered landscape is mirrored in scenes of stark, frozen beauty, but the slightest breeze, and this icy reflection of mountain and shore will be swept away.

▲

The tracks crisscrossing the snow were made by the small herd of reindeer in the distance. They are feeding on an area of exposed lichen, their staple diet, and will travel days in search of it. It will be many weeks before the sun has unfrozen enough of the ground for the animals to find food more easily.

▶

River ice piles up against the stunted pines on the banks of the River Tana, Norway's third longest river, famous for its record salmon. This spot is just north-east of Karasjok in the county of Finnmark, where the river forms the border between north Norway and Finnish Lapland.

◀

The beautiful, deserted Arctic coastline of Lille Porsangen, just south of latitude 70°45'. Dolphins and seals often swim into the fjord from the Arctic Ocean, an unforgettable sight. Here, even as early as March, the days are longer than in the south of Norway, and the midnight sun can be seen from mid-May until the end of July. But, from the end of November until the end of January, the sun never rises above the horizon.

▶

Small inshore fishing boats dot the harbour near Rypefjorden on the island of Kvaloya. Fishing is the economic foundation of the island, but in summer tourism plays its part as numerous travellers come to visit the world's most northerly town Hammerfest, which lies just north of here.

▲

About 3000 reindeer roam Mageroya. They are owned and herded by the Lapps of Karasjok. To reach these their summer grazing grounds, the adult animals have to swim the Mageroy Sound, the calves being ferried across in boats. In autumn the herds are returned to the mainland, where they migrate to their winter pastures.

◄

Honningsvag, at latitude 71°, on the Arctic island of Mageroya off Norway's northern coast, is west Finnmark's largest fishing village. From it a road lures the tourists north through rugged mountain terrain to their ultimate goal – the North Cape.

▲

The snow-streaked headland of Nordkapp (the North Cape) rises steeply from the Arctic Ocean to a height of 307 m (1,008 feet). At latitude 71°10′ 21″, it is traditionally the last piece of land in Europe, although actually the Knivskjellodden headland to the west extends another 24 m (79 feet) farther north.

▲

The midnight sun at the North Cape. Here the whole of the sun's disc can be seen at midnight from the middle of May until the end of July, but long before and long after these dates there is daylight around the clock. Severe gales can rage here for an average of 40 days each year, but this picture shows the Cape at its best, the way all travellers would like to see it, and a fitting end to their – and our – journey north.

──── **IMAGES OF NORWAY** ────